P9-EMG-215

CLASSIC
StoryTellers

MARK TWAIN

Mitchell Lane
PUBLISHERS

P.O. Box 196
Hockessin, Delaware 19707
www.mitchelllane.com

Titles in the Series

CLASSIC
StoryTellers

MARK TWAIN

Josepha Sherman

Printing   1   2   3   4   5   6   7   8

Library of Congress Cataloging-in-Publication Data

Sherman, Josepha.
   Mark Twain / by Joespha Sherman.
        p. cm — (Classic storytellers)
   Includes bibliographical references and index.
   ISBN 1-58415-374-1 (library bound)
1. Twain, Mark, 1835-1910—Juvenile literature 2. Authors, American—19th century
Biography—Juvenile literature. I. Title. II. Series.
PS1331.S46 2005
818'.409—dc22

                                                                    2004030263

ABOUT THE AUTHOR: Josepha Sherman is a professional fantasy and science fiction writer, a *Star Trek* novelist, a children's writer, and a nonfiction writer with over 60 books in print and over 150 short stories. She is also a professional folklorist and editor. In addition, she is a native New Yorker, has a degree in archaeology, loves to tinker with computers, follows the NY Mets ("wait till next year!"), and is a horse whisperer who has had a new foal fall asleep on her foot!

AUTHOR'S NOTE: This book is dedicated to the memory of Andre Norton/Alice Norton, a great lady of the science fiction community who we all still miss.

PHOTO CREDITS: Cover, pp. 1, 3, 6 Library of Congress; p. 10 Superstock; p. 14 Jamie Kondrchek; pp. 18, 23, 26 Library of Congress; p. 36 Associated Press

PUBLISHER'S NOTE: This story is based on the author's extensive research, which she believes to be accurate. Documentation of such research is contained on page 46-47.

The internet sites referenced herein were active as of the publication date. Due to the fleeting nature of some web sites, we cannot guarantee they will all be active when you are reading this book.

Contents

MARK TWAIN
Josepha Sherman

*For Your Information

StoryTellers StoryTellers StoryTellers StoryTellers StoryTellers StoryTellers StoryTellers StoryTellers

Mark Twain was one of America's best humorists. He is seen here in a contemporary drawing, standing on stage speaking to an audience. Behind him, his books fly about like paper birds.

Chapter 1

MARK TWAIN ON STAGE

On December 18, 1871, a happy group of men and women, ignoring the chill and gloom of a Chicago winter, chattered together as they entered the Michigan Avenue Baptist Church.

"Isn't this exciting?" a woman said to her husband. "We're actually going to hear Mark Twain speak. I've been truly looking forward to this."

"I wonder what he will talk about this time," a man said. "It will be something good and funny, I'm sure."

"It might be about his days as a miner."

"Or as a steamboat pilot. He was that, too, you know, on the Mississippi River, before the Civil War started."

"That's where he got his name," a woman whispered. "His real name isn't Mark Twain. It's Samuel Langhorne Clemens. *Mark Twain* is supposed to be a riverboat term."

"Didn't you see the advertisement? He said that he is going to speak about life out West."

The audience all settled into their seats and waited eagerly. Soon, to their excitement, Mark Twain appeared on stage. The audience thought he looked just fine, young and intelligent. His face, with its thick mustache drooping down on either side of his mouth, was as somber as that of a professor, but those seated close enough to the stage saw a humorous twinkle in his eyes. Twain this time was not wearing his trademark white suit, but because of the winter chill was in a black suit instead.

What happened next, and to the delight of the audience, was caught by a clever reporter from the *Chicago Tribune,* who noted audience reactions:

"Ladies and gentlemen," Twain began as though he were about to deliver a very scholarly talk. "By request of the Chairman of the committee, who has been very busy, and is very tired, I suppose, I ask leave to introduce to you the lecturer of the evening, Mr. Clemens, otherwise Mark Twain, a gentleman whose great learning, whose historical accuracy, whose devotion to science, and whose veneration for the truth [audience laughter] are only equaled by his moral character and his majestic presence [renewed audience laughter]. I refer these vague general terms to myself [audience giggling]. I am a little opposed to the custom of ceremoniously introducing the lecturer to the audience, because it seems to me unnecessary where the man has been properly advertised [audience laughter], and besides it is very uncomfortable for the lecturer. But where it is the custom, an introduction ought to be made, and I had rather make it myself in my own case, and then I can rely on getting in all the facts [continued audience laughter]."

The audience had a very good time that night.[1]

FYInfo

What's in a Name?

Many authors have used pseud-onyms, or fake names, in place of their real ones on their writings. There are many reasons for this. An author may have an important job and want to keep his name separate from his writing. If two authors have the same name, one of them may pick a pseudonym so that it's clear to the public who wrote what. Until the second half of the twentieth century, a woman author often had to take a male pseudonym or she wouldn't get published. The real name of science fiction author Andre Norton, for in-stance, is Alice Norton. She took the pseudonym because in the 1930s, when she started writing, no one wanted to publish science fiction books by a woman.

In the case of Mark Twain, the fake name and the real name seem to have been used almost at random. Not only was Samuel Clemens also Mark Twain, he also never seemed to have decided what signature was the "right" one.

On the letters he wrote to his mother and his brother Orion, he usually signed his name simply *Sam*. But things got more complicated when he was writing to others or signing autographs. In 1867, he signed a letter to Elisha Bliss, the publisher of the

Andre Norton/Alice Norton

American Publishing Company—which was publishing him as Mark Twain—*Sam. L. Clemens,* but in a series of letters to Elisha Bliss over the next two years, the signatures change to *Mark, Mark Twain,* and *Saml. L. Clemens.* By 1869, he was signing as *Clemens.*

But that wasn't the final solution, because in 1872, he signed a letter *Sam.l L. Clemens.* He also often signed letters to friends as *Mark.*

By 1896, he and his publishers seem to have worked out a double signature. From left to right is *S. L. Clemens,* and crossing that from lower left to upper right is *Mark Twain.*

At least there was no confusion on legal documents. On those, the signature is always a clear and uncomplicated *Samuel L. Clemens.*

What signature was his favorite? That is something no one knows.

The former home of Mark Twain in Hannibal, Missouri. It is now a museum. Notice the sign, celebrating one of his most famous characters, Tom Sawyer.

Chapter 2

THE "ALMOST INVISIBLE VILLAGE"

Usually the birth of a new baby is a happy event, but this birth wasn't very joyful. The baby boy who was born to John and Jane Clemens on November 30, 1835, was their sixth child, and he was frighteningly weak and possibly (the records aren't clear about this) premature. Even his mother thought that her poor, weak little baby was sure to die. What's more, the Clemens family was living in the tiny village of Florida, Missouri, which had only about a hundred people and nothing that could be called a medical facility. The boy would have to survive without much help.

Perhaps the most dramatic thing about the new child's birth was the appearance of Halley's comet in the sky just then. Maybe some of the family thought that it was a good omen, a sign that the boy, who was named Samuel, would live.

John Clemens was a lawyer who had met his wife-to-be while trying to help her family in court. It wasn't the best marriage. He was serious and somber, while she was cheerful and loved to laugh. As Sam later wrote, their marriage was "courteous . . . and respectful . . . they were always kind to each other, but . . . there was nothing warmer."[1]

The sickly boy, to his parents' surprise and relief, survived. Sadly, an older sister, Margaret, did not live. She died when Sam was not quite three.

Samuel Clemens describes his birthplace as "the almost invisible village of Florida, Monroe County, Missouri."[2] The village had only two streets, both of them unpaved and neither of them very long. They turned to thick mud in the rain, or thick dust in dry weather. There were only two stores, one of which was a general store run by Sam's uncle, John A. Quarles. The store sold a little bit of everything, including cloth, salt fish, coffee, brooms, rifles, and other supplies that people in a small country village might need.

Sam also gives a really good picture of the houses in a small town in 1835 Missouri. Most of the houses were log cabins, lit only by candles. He adds, "There was a log church. . . . The cracks between the logs were not filled . . . consequently, if you dropped anything smaller than a peach it was likely to go through. The church was perched upon short sections of logs, which elevated it two or three feet from the ground. Hogs slept under there, and whenever the dogs got after them during services, the minister had to wait till the disturbance was over. In winter there was always a refreshing breeze up through the

. . . floor; in summer there were fleas enough for all." During the week, the church building served as the village schoolhouse.[3]

In Missouri in those days, slavery was legal. Since John Clemens owned land, he would have needed farmworkers. At first he did own slaves, but soon after Sam's birth he changed over to using only hired workers instead. Whether this was done out of conscience or whether it was just easier to hire workers than to take care of slaves, no one knows. Pay in those days seems impossibly low, but the whole cost of living was much lower then. A teenage housemaid received $12 a year plus clothing, and an older housekeeper earned $25 a year plus clothing. A hired hand, a man who did hard farmwork, received over $75 dollars a year plus clothing.[4]

In 1838 John Clemens became a justice of the peace. There was no steady work for him in a place so small, and the town did not seem as if it was going to grow. When Sam was almost four, the Clemens family moved from tiny Florida to the somewhat larger town of Hannibal, Missouri, about thirty-five miles to the east. Hannibal had almost five hundred people. Located on the Mississippi River, it was already a growing port city, with steamboats constantly arriving or leaving from the other cities along the river, such as St. Louis and New Orleans.

Before there were airplanes or high-speed trains, steamboats were the major means of transportation up and down the 2,340-mile-long Mississippi River. Powered by steam engines, steamboats had twin smokestacks and wheels of paddles on their sides (making them side-wheelers) or sterns (making them paddle wheelers). They carried everything from people to animals and supplies.

Although steamboats are no longer a major way to travel, some still do exist. Here is the steamboat The Delta Queen *on the Mississippi River. It looks pretty much the way steamboats looked in Twain's day.*

In 1844, John Clemens settled his family into a two-story frame house at 206 Hill Street, a house that is still standing. Young Sam saw a good deal of the inside of this house in his early years, probably more than he wanted to see. Until age nine, he was still too weak and sickly to spend very much time out of doors. But by nine years old, he had finally grown strong enough to play outside and go to school.

Even with all the river traffic, Hannibal was a quiet town. Sam described it as the sort of small town where everyone knew everyone else and where people were friendly to one another. There was plenty of time for a boy to go fishing with his friends, play games, or just sit on a dock with his feet dangling and watching steamboats going up and down the river. That was when Sam fell in love with the mighty Mississippi, day-dreaming about what it would be like to work on one of those boats.

That was also where Sam and his friends almost killed someone by accident. On top of Holliday's Hill, overlooking Hannibal, sat a large boulder. Apparently it had looked ready to fall for years. Sam and his friends decided to help it a little. They loosened the earth around it, waiting for the boulder's great roll. What happened was even more spectacular than they had expected. The boulder went crashing and bounding down the hillside, flattening trees, crushing everything in its path. To the boys' horror, they saw a horse and wagon appear at the base of the hill. Were they about to see a terrible thing? To their great relief, the boulder took a great leap into the air, flew over the wagon, and landed with a crash, smashing a barrel-making shop but fortunately not killing anyone. The boys hurried away before anyone came to investigate, and no one knew that the boulder's journey had been anything but a natural accident—until Sam wrote about it many years later.

In 1847, tragedy struck the Clemens family. John Clemens died, probably of pneumonia. Although Sam's older brother, Orion Clemens, was already working for the *Western Union,* a Hannibal newspaper, money became very tight.

In 1848, when he was twelve, Sam left school to find work. There were no child labor laws back then to keep him from taking a job at that age. Sam became an apprentice to a printer named Joseph Ament at the *Missouri Courier* newspaper. An apprentice is someone who helps out a professional worker in exchange for learning how to do a job. In Sam's case, he learned about printing and how to do some general newspaper work. Two years later, in 1850, he joined Orion in a true job as an editorial assistant for the *Western Union.* His job required a lot more work than it would today. Today, computers take over a great deal of the tiresome job of typesetting and printing. In 1850, there was no such thing as computerized typesetting—or computers, for that matter. There were some typesetting machines in the larger cities, such as New York and Boston, but for most newspapers of that time, each letter had to be put into place by hand. Sam's new job included a range of tasks, from setting type to editing stories and even contributing sketches, or brief essays.

Over the next two years, Sam did so well in his job that he was able to take over for Orion when his older brother was temporarily called away from the paper on business. Not only did he make a good newspaperman, Sam even had some of his sketches published in 1852 in an important Philadelphia magazine, the *Saturday Evening Post.* He wasn't paid for those short pieces, but those were his first real publications. It was probably then that he realized just how much he enjoyed writing.

But Sam wasn't yet ready to take on writing as a career. There was too much in the world to see and do, he thought, to stay put long enough to write anything longer than a page or so.[5]

FYInfo

A Changing Outlook

The story of Mark Twain is a clear example of how someone can change for the better. The young Samuel Clemens was, without a doubt, a racist, referring to non-whites as "human vermin" in an 1853 letter. As he matured and learned more about life, he changed his opinions.

As he became an adult, Sam began to think more seriously and sympathetically about the hardships suffered by slaves, and to realize how tragic some of their stories were. He writes, "I vividly remember seeing a dozen black men and women chained to one another, once, and lying in a group on the pavement, awaiting shipment to the Southern slave market. Those were the saddest faces I have ever seen." In 1874 he wrote down and published the story of Mary Ann Cord, a former slave who told him how her husband and seven children had been sold away from her. Sam also paid scholarships to several African Americans so that they could go to college.[6]

Another major prejudice of Samuel Clemens's day was anti-Semitism, which is the hatred of Jews. Sam was definitely not an anti-Semite. In fact, he wrote in 1900 about himself with a touch of his cynical humor: "I think I have no color prejudices nor caste prejudices nor creed prejudices. Indeed, I know it. . . . All that I care to know is that a man is a human

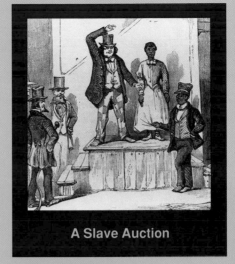

A Slave Auction

being—that is enough for me; he can't be any worse."[7]

A third prejudice of those days was against women, who in many cases weren't thought to be the equal of men. In the United States, women weren't even allowed to vote until 1920. Sam, however, thought that women deserved equal rights, and he supported a woman's right to vote. On January 20, 1901, he stated, "For twenty-five years I've been a woman's rights man. . . . I should like to see the time come when women shall help to make the laws. I should like to see that whiplash, the ballot, in the hands of women."[8]

Sam was also very strongly against cruelty to animals. In 1899, he angrily wrote about vivisections, which were surgical experiments performed on living creatures: "The pains [sic] which it inflicts upon unconsenting animals is the basis of my enmity towards it, and it is to me sufficient justification of the enmity without looking further."[9]

A young Mark Twain, before he became known for his books and lectures, sits between two other journalists. On the right is George Alfred Townsend, famous for his Civil War reports. On the left is David Gray, a newspaper writer and editor from Buffalo, New York.

Chapter 3

"MARK TWAIN" IS BORN

While Sam did learn his printing and writing skills in Hannibal, he was still too young to settle down. The boy was bored and restless. He didn't intend to stay in Hannibal all his life. He wanted to do more and see more.

In 1853, at age seventeen, Sam left Hannibal to take a printer's job in the city of St. Louis, farther down the Mississippi River. But he wasn't ready to settle down, so he left soon after he got there. Sam traveled east to New York and Philadelphia, working as a printer there, and sending his travel letters back to Hannibal to be published in the *Hannibal Journal.* Missing the Midwest, he came back in 1854 and worked with Orion in the town of Keokuk, Iowa, on Orion's new newspaper, the *Keokuk Journal.*

Sam was still restless. In 1857, when he was twenty-one, he found a fifty-dollar bill in the street, a great deal of money in those days. He went down to New Orleans, thinking that he would find a ship that could take him to South America. Instead, though, the Mississippi River lured him to stay. Sam writes, "When I was a boy, there was but one permanent ambition among my comrades. . . . That was, to be a steamboatman." That dream was still with him, and now he could do something about seeing it come true.[1]

The most important of the steamboatmen was not the captain but the pilot. The pilot had the job of safely navigating a steamboat through the Mississippi's tricky currents. While in New Orleans, Sam met a famous steamboat pilot named Horace Bixby. Sam convinced Bixby to take him on as his apprentice.

At first, the job didn't go too well. Bixby would call off "Six point" or "Nine point," which were vital river measurements. Sam failed to get the meaning of those calls. After struggling to control his temper at Sam's foolishness, Bixby told him, "My boy, you must get a little memorandum-book, and every time I tell you a thing, put it down right away. There's only one way to be a pilot, and that is to get this entire river by heart. You have to know it just like A B C."[2]

Sam spent the next two years doing just that—memorizing the entire river from St. Louis to New Orleans. In 1858, though, a family tragedy happened on the river. Sam's brother Henry was nineteen and also learning the steamboat trade. He was serving aboard the *Pennsylvania* when the *Pennsylvania*'s boiler exploded. Henry died in the accident. Sam mourned his brother. He felt guilty about Henry's death because he'd had an eerie feeling that something bad was going to happen to him.

Sam stayed with the river and earned his pilot's license on April 9, 1859. That must have been a wonderful day for him. Records show that he was an excellent pilot, constantly working and never once having an accident. His love for steamboats is clear in this description he gives of one about to dock:

> She is long and sharp and trim and pretty; she has two tall, fancy-topped chimneys, with a gilded device of some kind swung between them; a fanciful pilot-house, all glass and "gingerbread," perched on top of the [raised] deck behind them; the paddle-boxes are gorgeous with a picture or with gilded rays above the boat's name; the . . . [decks] are fenced and ornamented with clean white railings; there is a flag gallantly flying from the jack-staff; the furnace doors are open and the fires glaring bravely; . . . the captain stands by the big bell, calm, imposing, the envy of all; great volumes of the blackest smoke are rolling and tumbling out of the chimneys . . . an envied deckhand stands . . . with a coil of rope in his hand . . . the captain lifts his hand, a bell rings, the wheels stop; then they turn back, churning the water to foam, and the steamer is at rest.[3]

That happy career, the one he'd imagined for himself as a child, ended suddenly in 1861. That was the year that the U.S. Civil War between the North and the South began, catching Missouri in the middle of it. River traffic was shut down. The war ended in 1865 with the defeat of the South (and the end of slavery), but the steamboat business never recovered. The majestic ships were replaced by the less romantic but more efficient and less expensive tugboats and barges.

Sam seems to have been of two minds about serving in the war, probably because Missouri's people were also not sure which side to follow. He joined a volunteer militia group, the Marion Rangers, which was to serve the South, but the group disbanded without going to any battles. Then, in the middle of 1861, Orion got a commission from President Abraham Lincoln to become the Territorial Secretary of what was then the Nevada Territory. Sam went along on the adventure.

The excursion began uncomfortably. The brothers had to travel all the way to Nevada by stagecoach, which is basically a box on wheels pulled by a team of two to four horses. It may look like fun when one appears in a Western movie, but a real stagecoach had hard wooden seats and wooden wheels. There were no suspension springs, the way there are in a modern car, to keep passengers from feeling every jolt and bump in the long miles of unpaved road. The narrow interior had little room, and passengers were always bouncing into each other. It was a rough way to travel, and the Clemens brothers must have been really glad to reach their destination.

When Sam looked around the Nevada Territory, he found a wild, tough land of desert and mountains—and prospectors hunting for Nevada's rumored veins of gold and silver. The idea of making a fortune by mining struck Sam as a good one. He wandered all over the Nevada Territory for a year, trying to find the right spot to dig, the one that would yield up gold or silver. Finding nothing, he finally had to give up the mining life so that he could earn a living. For a time, he worked for a quartz min-

This stagecoach may look like something from a Western movie, but it's real. And this is the way people traveled in Samuel Clemens' day. He and his brother Orion would have ridden in one that looked pretty much like this one, complete with a four-horse team.

ing business, and he earned some extra money by sending humorous essays to the local newspaper, the *Virginia City Territorial Enterprise*. In 1862, he joined the paper as a full reporter.

In 1863, when he was also writing humor for the paper, Sam decided the time had come to use a pseudonym, a fake name, to separate his newspaper work from his fiction writing. His days as a steamboat pilot gave him the right pseudonym: Mark Twain. That may sound like a real name, but it is actually a river pilot's term. It means "measured to two fathoms deep"—two fathoms is about twelve feet. "Mark twain" is water that is deep enough for a boat to safely navigate.

In 1864, Sam took "Mark Twain" to San Francisco. He'd gotten into a violent argument with another editor that almost led to a duel using guns. When he learned that there were new laws against dueling, Sam left. He soon found a job with a San Francisco newspaper, the *Call*. He met other American authors, such as Bret Harte, who was already famous for his stories about California mining life, and who encouraged Sam to keep writing.

He did keep writing, as Mark Twain, and in 1865 he sold a short story, "The Celebrated Jumping Frog of Calaveras County," a humorous tale of a frog-jumping contest lost through a trick. The story appeared in the *New York Saturday Press* on November 18, 1865. What happened then was the type of sudden success that is the dream of many a writer. It became his breakout story, the story that swept the country and got his career as a writer truly started. Within months, the country knew about this mysterious Mark Twain and wanted to hear more from him.[4]

Sam was happy to help them out. There was a great deal of writing he meant to do, and now he had the encouragement he needed to do it.

FYInfo

The Duel

A duel is an old form of fighting that is arranged in advance and is fought by two people. The reason for a duel might be to avenge an Insult, to defend someone's honor, or to decide the winner of a prize such as land or the settlement of a boundary. Duels were usually fought with swords or guns, and traditionally the person being challenged to the duel had the choice of weapons.

Dueling, at least in Europe, may have begun around the seventh century A.D. as a way to settle legal disputes. It had been said that God strengthened the arm of the duelist who was in the right—but everyone must have realized that the better the duelist, the better chance he (rarely she) had to win. Pope Stephen VI outlawed judicial duels in 887.

A duel was usually very formal and followed special rules. The time and place had to be determined in advance, and the weapons chosen and agreed upon. Often, the duelists were allowed seconds, friends who served as aides but didn't actually fight or interfere. The point of a duel was not necessarily to kill one of the duelists, but merely to draw blood. The winner is the one who first wounds the other, or who comes away with fewer wounds after a set number of rounds.

In the United States, all different types of men dueled, including politi-

Aaron Burr

cians. Andrew Jackson often dueled, and in 1804 Aaron Burr killed founding father Alexander Hamilton in a duel. Dueling was outlawed in several states in the early 1800s, and across America by the late 1800s, as Clemens discovered. However, dueling continued until almost the twentieth century in the South and parts of the West.

Today, duels are usually fought just for sport. Viewers can watch the various types of sword duels (fencing) that take place at the summer Olympic Games. Duels can be seen in many movies, such as the 1961 medieval epic *El Cid,* in which two knights duel to the death, and in operas such as *Eugene Onegin,* by the nineteenth-century Russian composer Peter Tchaikovsky, in which a tragic and needless duel is fought to the death by two friends who have quarreled.

Mark Twain poses for his picture, taken somewhere between 1900 and 1910. He is shown wearing his trademark white suit.

Chapter 4

WRITER AND PERFORMER

Sam wasn't about to quit his newspaper work on the basis of the one story. He stayed on in San Francisco except for a four-month trip to Hawaii (then called the Sandwich Islands) in 1866, where he acted as a correspondent for another paper, the *Sacramento Union*. It was there, while writing a series of letters for publication, that a great idea came to him. Why not do humorous lectures? They sold very well in the nineteenth century.

As soon as he got back to California, Sam began arranging the first lecture tour for "Mark Twain," who was becoming a character that Sam played. Twain was a laid-back fellow with an easy way of speaking and a strong sense of humor. Sam writes of how much traveling was involved in this lecture tour: "I began as a lecturer in 1866, in California and Nevada; in 1867 lectured in New York once and in the Mississippi Valley a few times; in 1868 made the whole Western circuit; and in the two or three following seasons added the Eastern circuit to my route." It wasn't easy work, either. He says, "We had to bring out a new lecture every season." The lectures/storytelling performances were rehearsed the way actors rehearse shows now, performing them first in small towns. He explains: "[After] we had rehearsed about a month in those towns and made all the necessary corrections and revisings," he would move on to the big cities. "The country audience is the difficult audience. . . . A fair success in the country means a triumph in the city."[1]

After Sam had lectured in New York City in 1867, he went on to tour Europe and western Asia. That same year also saw the publication of his first book, *The Celebrated Jumping Frog of Calaveras County, and Other Sketches.*

Sam was already working on a new book in 1868, but he felt after all the traveling and public speaking he needed to take some time off to be with friends in Elmira, a town in upstate New York. One of the families that Sam visited was named the Langdons. He remembered seeing their daughter, Olivia, or Livy, eight months earlier, first in a miniature portrait, then in person. She was ten years younger than he, and he found her beautiful. On his visit, Sam had the chance to actually know Livy—and he fell madly in love with her almost on the spot. After only two weeks, he proposed marriage to her. Livy turned him down. Yes, she liked him—but two weeks was hardly enough time for so important a decision, she said.

She and Sam wrote back and forth over the months, and little by little, Livy's adoration grew. Sam was delighted to hear that she said over and over again that she loved him.

Before they could marry, Sam had to show her family that he was worthy of their daughter. He changed his lifestyle. No more swearing or rough behavior, he vowed, and no more wandering around the country at random! Sam went on a lecture tour for three months, writing love letters to Livy almost every night. Three months after that, they were engaged.

Sam's travels through Europe and western Asia turned out to be the basis of his next book, *Innocents Abroad,* published in 1869. Based on a collection of essays he'd written, this work took a humorous look at Americans visiting Europe. It quickly became a bestseller.

Sam married Livy on February 2, 1870, and the couple settled down in Buffalo, New York. Those who knew Sam were sure that he would want to go wandering again, but he stated firmly that he and his new wife were going to stay put. He liked the idea of settling down, and he and his wife were truly happy together. Unlike many men of his time, Sam was amused rather than upset that Livy wasn't a good cook.

Once settled, and with two people to support, he began to write in earnest. He produced columns for any publication that would pay, and he served as editor for the *Buffalo Express.* The public imagined Mark Twain as an easygoing fellow, even a lazy one. But the writer behind that image was another matter. Sam describes what writing was like: "Every day I nerve myself, and seize my pen and . . . prepare to . . . *work*. And then I pace the floor—back and forth, back and forth, with [empty] mind—and finally I lay down the pen and confess . . . that I am utterly empty. But I must work, and I *will* work. I will go straight at it and *force* it."[2]

Chapter 4   WRITER AND PERFORMER

Although Sam and Livy were still very happy together, tragedy nearly spoiled their first year as husband and wife. First, Livy's father died on August 6, 1870, after a long illness. This was almost as much of a shock to Sam as to Livy, since he had come to love her father, who had been kind and charming. Then one of Livy's girlhood friends, Emma Nye, collapsed and died in their house. Livy was pregnant at the time. Possibly from the strain Livy was feeling from the double tragedy, their first child, Langdon Clemens, was born prematurely on November 2, 1870. The weak and sickly child lived only two years. Even though poor Langdon had little chance of survival no matter how careful his parents were, Sam still blamed himself for the baby's death.

This sadness may have been the final blow that spurred Sam and Livy to move from Buffalo to Hartford, Connecticut. They both agreed that they badly needed a new start. In the 1870s, Hartford was one of the most successful cities in the Northeast. This did seem to be the right move for the young couple, and life soon grew calmer for Sam and Livy. It helped them that their neighbors were also professional writers who understood what the writing life was like. One of these neighbors was Harriet Beecher Stowe, who was famous for writing the 1852 antislavery novel *Uncle Tom's Cabin*.

In 1872 Sam published Mark Twain's new book, *Roughing It,* about his early adventures out West as a miner and reporter. Thanks to the success of *Innocents Abroad,* he had become one of the most popular comic speakers, and he took himself, as Mark Twain, on the lecture circuit—but only in the Northeast. Aside from one brief publicity trip to England in August, he stayed fairly close to home. He didn't want to get too far from Livy and their new child, a healthy little girl named Olivia Susan, or Susy, who had been born on March 19, 1872.

In 1873, Sam collaborated with another writer, neighbor Charles Dudley Warner, on his first novel, *The Gilded Age.* Unfortunately, it didn't sell very well—but Sam turned the work into a comedy that became one of the most successful plays of the 1870s. In the end, the story earned him more as a play than as a novel.

Clemens was, at least in the 1870s, a very happy man—at home. It was a bad time for the United States, which was still struggling to recover from the Civil War. Sam saw more and more examples of government corruption and gradually grew disgusted with his own country. After the trouble with *The Gilded Age,* he took Livy and Susy with him on a trip to England in 1873 and nearly decided to stay there. Instead, Sam and his family returned home. Sam expressed his feelings about the government with some sharp satire.

At the same time, Sam managed to escape his anger by starting to work on a book about boyhood in a small Missouri town. That book was to become one of his most famous: *The Adventures of Tom Sawyer.* It's full of fun and adventure, but it also gives the reader a good look at what Sam was like as a boy. While writing it, Sam learned more about himself and his creativity. Instead of forcing himself to write, as he had while in Buffalo, he said of the writing process, "When the [creative] tank runs dry, you've only got to leave it alone and it will fill up again."[3]

Meanwhile, Sam took a great deal of pleasure in watching Susy grow into an intelligent, curious, logical little girl. On June 8, 1874, she was joined by another daughter, Clara. The two sisters' play and quarrels amused their father; and he delighted in telling them stories.

The Adventures of Tom Sawyer was published in 1876, but because the publisher wasn't sure whether to market it as a boys' book or a book for adults, it failed to sell well at first. Sam had already been working on a sequel, *The Adventures of Huckleberry Finn,* but the news that *Tom Sawyer* wasn't selling well stopped him cold.

The discouragement of the late 1870s didn't stop Sam from writing, though. In 1880, *A Tramp Abroad* was published. It told of his fictionalized travels through Germany and the Swiss Alps. Sam didn't hide the fact that he'd written it strictly to make money—and it made a good deal of money, selling very well.

He and Livy's third and final child, Jean, was born in 1880. Around the time of her birth, Sam had been plotting out a children's historical novel. It would be set in the time of King Henry VIII, about a prince and a poor boy who look like twins and switch places. He wasn't sure that *The Prince and the Pauper* fit the Mark Twain name, but after the success of *A Tramp Abroad,* it was published by "Mark Twain" in 1882.

Life on the Mississippi came next, in 1883. This book contained Sam's memories of life as a riverboat pilot, and it, too, sold well.

Mark Twain's success was beginning to worry Sam. He wrote, "I am frightened at the proportions of my prosperity."

He worried that just as quickly as fame had come, it might leave.[4]

By this time he had finished the sequel to *Tom Sawyer.* *Huckleberry Finn* was published in 1884, and many people think that it is Sam's finest book. Huck Finn was a character in the first book, a boy who is a good person yet lives outside what is considered right and proper by most people. Sam based him in part or maybe even totally on a real boy, Tom Blankenship, whom he had known in Hannibal, Missouri. He writes, "In Huckleberry Finn I have drawn Tom Blankenship exactly as he was. He was ignorant, unwashed, insufficiently fed; but he had as good a heart as ever any boy had. . . . He was the only really independent person—boy or man—in the community, and by consequence he was tranquilly and continuously happy and envied by the rest of us. And as his society was forbidden us by our parents . . . we sought and got more of his society than any other boy's."[5]

In the book, Huck flees his abusive father and, together with the runaway slave, Jim, escapes by raft down the Mississippi River. In the book, the reader sees both the good and the bad in people, and the conflicts between doing what society expects and what is the right thing. Some people have thought that, because of the treatment of African Americans in it, there is racism in *Huckleberry Finn,* but others think that Sam would not have written anything racist, not at that stage of his life, and was instead trying to show racism for the wrong that it is.

Meanwhile, Sam continued his lecture circuit. Susy saw her father perform one of his lectures, and at age thirteen wrote a review. In it, she says, "When he came out onto the stage, I remember the people behind me exclaimed, 'Isn't he funny!' . . . I thought papa was very funny."

In 1884, Sam also started up a new publishing business, Charles L. Webster and Company. The company published Mark Twain's works, such as *A Connecticut Yankee in King Arthur's Court,* a comic and cynical look at medieval England. The company also published works of other writers, including American general and president Ulysses S. Grant. Unfortunately, Sam and his company failed after much of the company money was lost in a bad investment. They had placed their bets on an automatic typesetting machine that didn't actually work. Charles L. Webster and Company went bankrupt in 1894, and Sam was left with a great deal of debt.

Sam took his family with him to Europe in 1895. For several years, the family moved around from France to Germany, Italy, and Switzerland. Sam continued lecturing to help pay off his debts. He also wrote *Following the Equator,* a book based on the family's travels. It would be published in 1897; the debt would finally be paid off in 1898.

In 1896, the family returned to Hartford. Susy had become ill with a dangerous disease called meningitis. She died that year in August.

Sam and Livy were heartsick with grief. The loss of their daughter was almost more than they could bear.

FYInfo

Books by Subscription

In Samuel Clemens's day, books were sold in two different ways. There were bookstores, just as there are now, but there weren't many of them. Scores of towns and even cities didn't have bookstores; neither were there any in rural areas. The other method was selling books "by subscription only," which was how most of Mark Twain's works were sold.

Books "sold by subscription only" were sold by a sales agent who called on people at their homes or offices. Until the 1890s, thousands of such agents went door to door throughout the cities and towns of the United States. Many of the agents were Civil War veterans, although there were some women agents too. While some sold only books, others sold brushes, kitchen utensils, and just about anything else a home might need. These salespeople were especially useful in areas where there weren't any nearby cities. Those were the days before there were such things as shopping malls. Few people could afford automobiles or had the time for a long drive over rutted roads to get to stores in towns or cities.

The prices charged for books sold by subscription were much higher than for those sold in stores. This

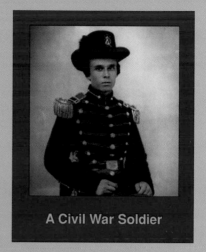

A Civil War Soldier

gave Mark Twain a higher income than Sam had expected, and made him very happy about the process.

Many publishers, though, disagreed, since they felt they had no control over the books once they were in the hands of sales agents. Not surprisingly, the bookstore owners also objected. Some authors didn't like the subscription process either, saying that all it did was make books objects to be sold whether they were good or not.

As Sam's writing career continued, he saw the subscription system fade. By the 1890s, books were being sold as they are today, mostly through bookstores. Sales agents became sales representatives, selling the books not to readers but to bookstore owners.

Mark Twain shown with his wife Olivia (center) and daughter Clara (left) at their suburban London home in 1900. The family doesn't look very happy. But that was because it was fashionable for those being photographed to look thoughtful.

Chapter 5

THE NEW CENTURY

Sam kept on writing through the end of the nineteenth century, although his later works never were quite as popular as the earlier ones. They included *The Tragedy of Pudd'nhead Wilson,* which tackled racial inequalities with bitter humor, in 1894, and *Personal Recollections of Joan of Arc,* a cynical look at the Joan of Arc story, in 1896.

At the turn of the twentieth century, Sam, as Mark Twain, spent most of his time lecturing in New York City. He also received two honorary degrees, one in 1901 from Yale University in New Haven, Connecticut, and the other in 1902 from the University of Missouri. He had come to be considered a famous celebrity in a time before television and the Internet make instant stars who quickly disappear. Sam was almost always on call at sites ranging from New York's famous Carnegie Hall and Barnard College to private clubs such as the Players.

He served as a toastmaster on many occasions. Everyone owned, or claimed to own, at least some of his books.

Then life started to turn around for Sam. Livy became seriously ill in 1903; her doctor advised her to move to a warmer climate. She moved to Florence, Italy. Sam couldn't visit her as often as he would have liked, since his career kept him in the United States, but he was there at her bedside when Livy died in June 1904. Heartbroken, Sam wrote, "An hour ago, the best heart that ever beat for me and mine went silent out of this house, and I am as one who wanders and has lost his way."[1]

In 1905, Sam turned seventy. His publishers organized a big birthday party for him that attracted almost two hundred of America's most important writers and editors. Sam by this point had made Mark Twain into a special figure. He had flowing white hair, a full white mustache, and almost always wore a white flannel suit whenever he went out. To the public, he seemed untouched by his family tragedies.

The image was far from the truth. Unable to stand the idea of living in the same house without Livy, Sam moved to a house on New York's Fifth Avenue. There, he continued to write— and to play his favorite game, billiards, for hours.

Sam spent most of the first ten years of the twentieth century in New York City. He used his fame to speak out against injustice. He became a reformer, using his writing to attack corrupt government, the lynch mobs of the South— people who saw the hanging of ex-slaves without trial or judge as just and even entertaining—and anyone else who tried denying people of their rights.

The books that Sam wrote after Livy's death were often cynical and bitter. *Extracts from Adam's Diary* appeared in 1904, and *Eve's Diary* and *What Is Man?* were published in 1906. *Chapters from My Autobiography* was published in 1907, the year he received another honorary degree, this time from Oxford University; and *Letters from the Earth* came out in 1909.

By this time his strength was giving out. In 1908, Sam moved to Redding, Connecticut, to a house he named Stormfield, after one of his characters. At first things seemed to be going well. A neighbor, Dan Beard, describes Sam's arrival there: "The announcement that Mark Twain was to arrive on the afternoon train was received with joyful anticipation, and [people] turned out to meet him, with their carriages, buckboards, and surreys decorated with flowers, old-fashioned pink roses, and pink ribbons, and filled with neatly dressed children. . . . When the famous author alighted from the train . . . the photographer was there. . . . After posing for the picture Mr. Clemens got into the surrey, which the ladies had beautifully decorated with dainty maidenhair ferns and pink roses, and drove to his new home, escorted by his new neighbors."[2]

In 1909, on Christmas Eve, Sam's youngest daughter, Jean, died of an epileptic seizure. Feeling utterly alone and sad, Sam wrote a memorial to her, *The Death of Jean*, and vowed never to write again. He surrounded himself with what he called his Angelfish, a group of young girls who, he said, if things had been different, would have been his grandchildren. Sam liked the cheerfulness and energy of the youngsters, probably because he'd been the father of three girls, and said about them, "The average American girl possesses the valuable qualities of naturalness, honesty, and inoffensive straightforwardness; she is nearly barren of troublesome conventions and artificialities; consequently, her presence and her ways are unembarrassing, and one is acquainted with her and on the pleasantest terms with her before he knows how it came about."[3]

Sam knew that death was on the way, and wasn't really afraid of it. He said in 1909, "I came in with Halley's comet in 1835. It is coming again next year, and I expect to go out with it. It will be the greatest disappointment of my life if I don't go out with Halley's comet. The Almighty said, no doubt: 'Now here are these two unaccountable freaks; they came in together, they must go out together.'"[4]

That was exactly what happened. On April 21, 1910, Sam Clemens, "Mark Twain," died—and Halley's comet was bright in the sky.

Today, he is still famous, and his books are considered classics. All over the country are memorials, from his childhood home in Hannibal, Missouri, which is open to the public; to Calaveras County, California, which holds the Calaveras County Fair and Jumping Frog Jubilee every third weekend in May; to walking tours in New York City that cover places Twain visited.

Sam Clemens has truly become Mark Twain, not just a writer, but a part of America.

FYInfo

Mark Twain, Pop Culture Star

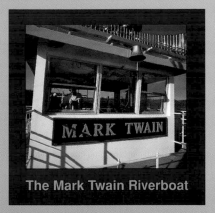

The Mark Twain Riverboat

Many popular authors soon find their books being collected, from first editions to autographed copies to rare articles. Mark Twain was no exception.

He also became a pop hero, with his name borrowed or downright stolen to advertise hotels or to market games, new trains, or brands of flour. Sometimes his name was added to other authors' works who were attempting to publicize their own works. After his death, his characters appeared in comic books and movies. A recent appearance of a Mark Twain character outside of his works was in the 2003 fantasy adventure movie, *The League of Extraordinary Gentlemen.* Based on a comic book series, the movie features Tom Sawyer as a government agent.

His own image and the Mark Twain personality became commercialized, too. As early as the 1920s, he was being represented in a series of collectible dolls, and his image, complete with the typical white suit, can still be found gracing T-shirts, refrigerator magnets, and greeting cards.

Sam had given Mark Twain such a distinctive voice and style that he seems a natural target for impersonators. Many modern actors have re-created Mark Twain as a performer. Mark Twain is the protagonist, or the lead character, of several novels, too. There is Kirk Mitchell's *Never the Twain*

(Ace Books, New York). Peter J. Heck's series of mystery novels stars Mark Twain as a detective: *Death on the Mississippi, A Connecticut Yankee in Criminal Court, The Prince and the Prosecutor, Tom's Lawyer, The Mysterious Strangler,* and *The Guilty Abroad* (all from Berkeley Prime Crime, New York). Strangest of Mark Twain's fictional appearances is in Philip José Farmer's fantasy *Riverworld* series, in which Twain appears in another world and dimension (Penguin Putnam, New York).

Several associations and societies exist to study and discuss Mark Twain and his works. These include the Mark Twain Circle of New York, part of the larger Mark Twain Circle of America, which holds panels about Twain at the annual conferences of the Modern Language Association. The Mark Twain Forum is a scholarly e-mail list. There is even the Japan Mark Twain Society, which furthers the study and reading of Mark Twain in Japan.

CHRONOLOGY

1835	Born in Florida, Missouri, on November 30; Halley's comet is visible in the sky
1839	Clemens family moves to Hannibal, Missouri
1847	John Clemens dies
1848	Apprentices to Joseph Ament at the *Missouri Courier*
1850	Works for brother Orion on *Western Union* newspaper
1852	First publications, including first paid story, "The Dandy Frightening the Squatter"
1859	Earns river pilot license
1861	Civil War shuts down travel on the Mississippi
1862	Becomes a reporter for Nevada's *Virginia City Territorial Enterprise*
1864	Moves to California to work on the *San Francisco Call*
1865	Tries mining for gold
1866	Reports from Hawaii for the *Sacramento Union*
1870	Marries Olivia Langdon
1871	First child, Langford, dies; moves to Hartford, Connecticut
1872	Daughter Olivia Susan "Susy" Clemens is born
1874	Second daughter, Clara Clemens, is born
1880	Last child, Jean Clemens, is born
1890	Mother, Jane Clemens, dies
1895	Embarks on round-the-world lecture tour to pay off debts
1896	Daughter Susan dies
1904	Wife, Olivia, dies
1908	Moves to Redding, Connecticut
1909	Daughter Jean dies
1910	Dies April 21; Halley's comet is visible in the sky

SELECTED WORKS

1852	*The Dandy Frightening the Squatter*
1867	*The Celebrated Jumping Frog of Calaveras County, and Other Sketches*
1869	*Innocents Abroad*
1872	*Roughing It*
1873	*The Gilded Age* (with Charles Dudley Warner)
1876	*The Adventures of Tom Sawyer*
1880	*A Tramp Abroad*
1882	*The Prince and the Pauper*
1883	*Life on the Mississippi*
1884	*The Adventures of Huckleberry Finn*
1889	*A Connecticut Yankee in King Arthur's Court*
1892	*The American Claimant*
1893	*The 1,000,000 Pound Bank Note*
1894	*The Tragedy of Pudd'nhead Wilson*
	Tom Sawyer Abroad
1896	*Tom Sawyer, Detective*
1897	*Following the Equator*
1900	*The Man That Corrupted Hadleyburg*
1902	*A Double-Barrelled Detective Story*
1904	*Extracts from Adam's Diary*
1906	*What Is Man?*
1909	*Letters from the Earth*
	The Death of Jean

TIMELINE IN HISTORY

1803	The Louisiana Purchase doubles the size of the new United States.
1835	Halley's comet appears.
1836	The Alamo falls in San Antonio, Texas.
1844	Samuel Morse patents the telegraph.
1846	United States claims California and fights Mexico.
1848	Gold is discovered in California.
1852	Harriett Beecher Stowe publishes her antislavery novel, *Uncle Tom's Cabin*.
1860	Abraham Lincoln is elected president; the Southern states begin to leave the United States.
1861–1865	The Civil War is waged.
1863	President Lincoln signs the Emancipation Proclamation.
1865	President Lincoln is assassinated.
1868	Ulysses S. Grant is elected president.
1869	The country is linked by the transcontinental railroad.
1876	Alexander Graham Bell patents the telephone.
1879	Thomas Edison invents the lightbulb.
1898	The Spanish-American War is waged.
1903	The Wright brothers complete the first manned, powered flight.
1904	Work begins on the Panama Canal.
1909	The National Association for the Advancement of Colored People is founded.
1914	World War I begins.
1918	World War I ends.

CHAPTER NOTES

Chapter One
Mark Twain on Stage

1. "Mark Twain," *The Chicago Tribune,* 20 December 1871, http://etext.lib.virginia.edu/railton/roughingit/lecture/rilectct.html

Chapter Two
The "Almost Invisible Village"

1. Walter Blair, ed., *Mark Twain's Hannibal, Huck & Tom* (Berkeley: University of California Press, 1969), p. 39.

2. Mark Twain, *Autobiography of Mark Twain*, edited by Charles Neider (New York: Harper & Brothers, 1959), p. 1.

3. Ibid.

4. Ibid., pp. 2–3.

5. Ron Powers, *Dangerous Water: A Biography of the Boy Who Became Mark Twain*, (New York: Basic Books, 1999), pp. 167–173.

6. Mark Twain, *Autobiography of Mark Twain*, edited by Charles Neider (New York: Harper & Brothers, 1959), pp. 30–31.

7. Mark Twain, from *The Man That Corrupted Hadleyburg, and Other Stories and Essays* (New York: Harper & Brothers, 1900), p. 254.

8. Mark Twain, "Votes for Women," speech given at the annual meeting of the Hebrew Technical School for Girls, January 20, 1901, at *Social Justice Speeches,* http://www.edchange.org/multicultural/speeches/twain_votes.html

9. Mark Twain, "Letter to the London Anti-Vivisection Society," at http://www.twainquotes.com/Vivisection.html

Chapter Three
"Mark Twain" Is Born

1. Mark Twain, *Life on the Mississippi*, included in *Mississippi Writings* (New York: Literary Classics of the United States, Inc., 1982), p. 253.

2. Ibid., p. 265.

3. Ibid., pp. 330–331.

4. Justin Kaplan, *Mark Twain and His World* (New York: Simon and Schuster, 1974), p. 59.

Chapter Four
Writer and Performer

1. Mark Twain, *Autobiography of Mark Twain*, edited by Charles Neider (New York: Harper & Brothers, 1959), pp. 161–166.

2. Ibid., p. 265.

3. Ibid.

4. Albert Bigelow Paine, *Mark Twain, a Biography, 1875–86,* at http://www.fullbooks.com/Mark-Twain-A-Biography-1875-865.html

5. Mark Twain, *Autobiography of Mark Twain*, edited by Charles Neider (New York: Harper & Brothers, 1959), p. 68.

Chapter Five
The New Century

1. Mark Twain, *Autobiography of Mark Twain*, edited by Charles Neider (New York: Harper & Brothers, 1959), p. 329.

2. Dan Beard, "Mark Twain as a Neighbor," *American Monthly Review of Reviews,* vol. 41, June 1910.

3. Mark Twain, *The American Claimant,* chapter 20; first published 1892; quoted from http://www.readbookonline.net/read/2/76/

4. Albert Bigelow Paine, *Mark Twain, a Biography: The Personal and Literary Life of Samuel Langhorne Clemens* (New York: Harper & Brothers, 1912), vol. 3.

FURTHER READING

For Young Adults

Aller, Susan. *Mark Twain*. Minneapolis: Lerner Publications, 2001.

Cox, Clinton. *Mark Twain: America's Humorist, Dreamer, Prophet*. New York: Scholastic, 1997.

Quackenbush, Robert M. *Mark Twain? What Kind of a Name Is That?* Englewood Cliffs, New Jersey: Prentice Hall, 1984.

Works Cited

Anderson, Frederick, ed. *Mark Twain's Notebook & Journals*. 3 volumes. Berkeley: University of California Press, 1975–1979.

Beard, Dan. "Mark Twain as a Neighbor," *American Monthly Review of Reviews*. Vol. 41, June 1910.

Blair, Walter, ed. *Mark Twain's Hannibal, Huck & Tom*. Berkeley: University of California Press, 1969.

Branch, Edgar Marquess, ed. *Mark Twain's Letters*. 5 volumes. Berkeley: University of California Press, 1988–1997.

Brashear, Minnie M. *Mark Twain: Son of Missouri*. New York: Russell & Russell, 1964.

Clemens, Clara. *My Father, Mark Twain*. New York: Harper & Brothers, 1931.

DeVoto, Bernard, ed. *Mark Twain in Eruption*. New York: Harper & Brothers, 1922.

———. *Mark Twain's America*. Boston: Little, Brown, 1932.

Fatout, Paul. *Mark Twain on the Lecture Circuit*. Bloomington, Indiana: Indiana University Press, 1960.

Hoffman, Andrew. *Inventing Mark Twain*. New York: William Morrow and Company, 1997.

Kaplan, Justin. *Mark Twain and His World*. New York: Simon and Schuster, 1974.

Kaplan, Justine. *Mr. Clemens and Mark Twain*. New York: Simon and Schuster, 1966.

Neider, Charles, ed. *The Autobiography of Mark Twain*. New York: Harper and Brothers, 1959.

Neider, Charles, ed. *Papa: An Intimate Biography of Mark Twain by His Thirteen-Year-Old Daughter Suzy*. New York: Doubleday, 1985.

Paine, Albert Bigelow. *Mark Twain, a Biography: The Personal and Literary Life of Samuel Langhorne Clemens*. 3 volumes. New York: Harper and Brothers, 1912.

Powers, Ron. *Dangerous Water: A Biography of the Boy Who Became Mark Twain*. New York: Basic Books, 1999.

Rasmussen, R. Kent. *Mark Twain A–Z: The Essential Reference to His Life and Writings*. Oxford and New York: Oxford University Press, 1995.

Scott, Arthur L. *Mark Twain at Large*. Chicago: Henry Regnery Company, 1969.

Steinbrink, Jeffrey. *Getting to Be Mark Twain*. Berkeley and Los Angeles: University of California Press, 1991.

Twain, Mark. *Autobiography of Mark Twain,* edited by Charles Neider. New York: Harper and Brothers, 1959.

Twain, Mark. *Letters to His Publishers,* edited by Hamlin Hill. Berkeley and Los Angeles: University of California Press, 1967.

Twain, Mark. *Life on the Mississippi*. Included in *Mississippi Writings*. New York: Literary Classics of the United States, 1982.

FURTHER READING CONT'D

Twain, Mark. *The Man That Corrupted Hadleyburg, and Other Stories and Essays.* New York: Harper and Brothers, 1900.

Twain, Mark. "Votes for Women," speech given at the annual meeting of the Hebrew Technical School for Girls, January 20, 1901.

Wecter, Dixon. *Sam Clemens of Hannibal: The Formative Years of America's Great Indigenous Writer.* Boston: Houghton Mifflin Company, 1961.

On the Internet

The Mark Twain Circle of New York
http://salwen.com/mtahome.html

The Mark Twain Papers and Project
http://bancroft.berkeley.edu/MTP/about.html

Mark Twain Quotations, Newspaper Collections, and Related Resources
http://www.twainquotes.com

"The History of Dueling in America"
http://www.pbs.org/wgbh/amex/duel/sfeature/dueling.html

GLOSSARY

autobiography
(aw-teh-by-AH-greh-fee)
someone's life story, written by him or herself.

autograph
(AW-teh-graf)
a signature, often by someone famous.

Civil War
a war between the Northern and Southern states of the United States, fought between 1861 and 1865.

flannel
(FLAH-nel)
a soft cotton or wool fabric often used in suits.

Halley's comet
(HAH-leez KAH-met)
a bright body of ice and dust that has an orbit, or circular path through space, that brings it in sight of Earth once approximately every seventy-five years.

paddle wheeler
a steamboat with one wheel of paddles at the stern, or back.

reformer
(re-FOR-mer)
someone who tries to change things for the better.

satire
(SAH-tire)
humorous writing intended to make fun of something or someone.

side-wheeler
a steamboat with a wheel of paddles on each side.

steamboat
a boat that gets its power from steam engines.

typesetter
(TYPE-seh-ter)
a person who prepares stories for print. The typesetter puts the letters (which are cut from wooden blocks or metal plates) into place so that they can be inked, then printed as a book or newspaper. Modern typesetting is usually done by computer.

INDEX